AF228550

TEEN CHALLENGES

ACADEMIC ANXIETY

by Carla Mooney

CONTENT CONSULTANT

Jerrell C. Cassady, PhD
Professor of Psychology
Department of Educational Psychology
Ball State University

An Imprint of Abdo Publishing | abdobooks.com

ABDOBOOKS.COM

Published by Abdo Publishing, a division of ABDO, PO Box 398166, Minneapolis, Minnesota 55439. Copyright © 2022 by Abdo Consulting Group, Inc. International copyrights reserved in all countries. No part of this book may be reproduced in any form without written permission from the publisher. Essential Library™ is a trademark and logo of Abdo Publishing.

Printed in the United States of America, North Mankato, Minnesota.
102021
012022

Cover Photo: Antonio Diaz/Shutterstock Images
Interior Photos: Antonio Diaz/Shutterstock Images, 4; Shutterstock Images, 10–11, 17, 30, 36, 44, 50, 57, 60, 62, 82, 86, 95, 98; Iakov Filimonov/Shutterstock Images, 12, 69; Bronson Chang/Shutterstock Images, 22; Wave Break Media/Shutterstock Images, 24; New Africa/Shutterstock Images, 35; iStockphoto, 43, 48; Rawpixel.com/Shutterstock Images, 47; Antonio Guillem/Shutterstock Images, 55, 90; Photographee.eu/Shutterstock Images, 65; Monkey Business Images/iStockphoto, 71; Africa Studio/Shutterstock Images, 74; Dragon Images/Shutterstock Images, 78; Monkey Business Images/Shutterstock Images, 85

Editor: Katharine Hale
Series Designer: Colleen McLaren

LIBRARY OF CONGRESS CONTROL NUMBER: 2021941172

PUBLISHER'S CATALOGING-IN-PUBLICATION DATA

Names: Mooney, Carla, author.

Title: Academic anxiety / by Carla Mooney

Description: Minneapolis, Minnesota : Abdo Publishing, 2022 | Series: Teen challenges | Includes online resources and index.

Identifiers: ISBN 9781532196249 (lib. bdg.) | ISBN 9781098218058 (ebook)

Subjects: LCSH: High school students--Juvenile literature. | Test anxiety--Juvenile literature. | Stress in adolescence--Juvenile literature. | Academic achievement--Juvenile literature. | Achievement motivation in adolescence--Juvenile literature.

Classification: DDC 373.1821--dc23

CONTENTS

Trigger warning: This chapter presents a scenario of attempted suicide.

Many people with academic anxiety struggle to take tests.

CHAPTER ONE

TEST TIME

At the beginning of a statistics exam, Georgia suddenly broke out into a cold, clammy sweat. The high school junior's stomach churned, and she felt nauseous. She quickly glanced around the classroom. All around her, students hunched over their desks and scribbled answers onto their papers.

Georgia looked back at the questions on her test paper. Although she had spent days studying the material, now she could not remember what to do. All she could think was, "I'm going to fail this test." A feeling of panic quickly built inside her. Her heart was beating so loudly, Georgia was certain that her classmates could hear it.

When Georgia began to feel light-headed and dizzy, she forced herself to focus on her breathing. She took several slow, deep breaths while she counted to 50. Then she closed her eyes and silently repeated a mantra to herself: "I don't have to be perfect." Her heart rate began to drop, and her breathing returned to normal. Georgia soon felt calm enough to tackle the test. She remembered how to solve the first problem and began to write down her answer.

STRESS AT SCHOOL

Everyone experiences stress and anxiety in school for a variety of reasons. Some students feel stressed when they have to give a presentation in front of the class. Others become anxious before a big test. Many students feel stressed out when they are working on a subject that is not their strongest, or when it takes longer to finish an assignment or project than they had anticipated. Some students even worry every time they enter the classroom of a strict or unpleasant teacher. These feelings of stress and anxiety related to school pressures are called academic anxiety.

For most people, these feelings of pressure, stress, and anxiety at school pass quickly. For others, they linger and become something more serious. For these people, academic anxiety can affect how they think and feel about the world around them. Academic anxiety can interfere with a person's daily life and ability to function in school.

A PROBLEM ON THE RISE

Increasingly, children and teens across the United States are struggling with the pressures they face at school. According to a 2018 survey by the Pew Research Center—a nonpartisan organization that researches current issues, attitudes, and trends in the world—teens put academics at the top of the list of pressures they face. In the Pew survey, 61 percent of teens said that they felt "a lot" of pressure to get good grades while an

STRESS: A NORMAL REACTION

In some situations, stress is good. Stress is the body's normal reaction to a change that requires a person to adjust or respond. Stress can be generated by something in the environment or the body, or by a person's thoughts. The body's autonomic nervous system responds to stress with physiological changes that allow the body to quickly react. It triggers the body's fight-or-flight response. This response prepares the body to take action when it perceives a potential threat. A person's heart rate and breathing rate increase. Blood flow to the muscles increases, and the pupils dilate. These changes allow the body to respond quickly—either to fight the threat or flee from the danger. They keep a person alert and motivated, allowing them to perform well under pressure and avoid danger.

WHEN STRESS BECOMES UNHEALTHY

Everyone deals with stress from time to time. However, when stress continues over a long period of time, the elevated stress hormones can have a negative effect on the body. People dealing with chronic stress may experience physical problems such as headaches, nausea, increased blood pressure, chest pain, and changes in sleep habits. They may also develop emotional problems such as depression, anxiety disorders, and panic attacks. Too much stress may also have a long-term effect on the body. Research has linked stress to several leading causes of death, including heart disease, cancer, and lung disease.

additional 27 percent said they felt "some" pressure to get good grades. The pressure youth feel to do well in school may be tied to their plans after graduation. According to the same survey, nearly 60 percent of teens said that they planned to attend a four-year college after high school. These college-bound teens are more likely than those who do not plan to attend a four-year college to say they feel a lot of pressure to do well in school.[2]

For many teens, this academic pressure can lead to problems with anxiety disorders and depression. In fact, according to the same Pew survey, seven out of ten teens believe that anxiety and depression among their peers are major problems.[3] Laurie Farkas, former director of student services for Northampton public schools in Massachusetts, has noticed an increase in students struggling with anxiety. "We've always had kids who didn't want to come in the door or who were worried about things. But there's just been a steady increase of severely anxious students," Farkas said.[4]

Academic anxiety is also growing in America's colleges and universities. In 2019, two-thirds of college students reported feeling overwhelming anxiety in the past 12 months, according to the National College Health Assessment—an increase from 50 percent in 2011. And nearly 30 percent of those students reported that their anxiety affected their academic performances.[5]

SCHOOL REFUSAL

Sometimes anxiety disorders in children and teens result in a reluctance to go to school. Children may beg to be excused from school, complain of being sick, or even run home when forced to go to school. School refusal is based in fear—often fear of school or fear of leaving home. It can be triggered by an illness, a stressful event, or even the beginning of a new school year. School refusal can be a serious problem. To overcome it, parents and mental health counselors must treat the underlying worries and fears that drive a child to avoid school. Often, a team of counselors, parents, and teachers will develop a behavioral plan for the child. They might also put together a support system of people the child can turn to when he or she feels afraid or anxious at school.

Yet there is hope. Many people who experience academic anxiety learn to successfully manage their symptoms with a combination of treatment and lifestyle changes. They surround themselves with a strong support system that can help during difficult times, and they are able to lead happy and productive lives.

Students can overcome academic anxiety to thrive in school.

Too much pressure from parents to do well in school can cause academic anxiety.

CHAPTER TWO

WHAT IS ACADEMIC ANXIETY?

Everyone experiences anxiety at some point in their lives. For some teens, the pressure of school can trigger feelings of anxiety. Students worry about not doing well in class, not getting into the college of their dreams, and failing to live up to the expectations of their parents, teachers, and peers. "Many students struggle with being defined by their grades and their test scores. Because a student's GPA and test scores are a large portion of college admissions, even more pressure is put on students to do well," says Kelly Bergmann, a guidance counselor at Iowa City West High School. "Obviously this creates more anxiety."[1]

WHAT IS ANXIETY?

Anxiety is one of the body's natural emotional responses to stress. It is a feeling of fear or apprehension about something that may happen in the future. For many

HISTORY OF ANXIETY

For many years, anxiety disorders were not well understood by the medical community. Before 1980, doctors diagnosed people experiencing an anxiety disorder with a case of "stress" or "nerves." Because there was little understanding of these disorders by doctors, few people received effective treatment for anxiety. Instead, early treatments included herbs and balms, bathing in very cold rivers and streams, applying extreme temperatures to the body, and bloodletting with leeches. Later treatments included psychoanalysis and medications. Anxiety disorders were officially recognized by the American Psychiatric Association in 1980. Since the recognition of anxiety disorders as diagnosable mental disorders, researchers have shown more interest in finding effective treatments for anxiety. Today, many anxiety disorders can be prevented or lessened with early diagnosis and effective treatment.

people, giving a speech in public, going to a job interview, or even the first day of school can make them feel nervous and afraid. Many life events, such as going on a first date or starting a new job, can also cause feelings of anxiety.

Normal anxiety can be beneficial in many cases. For example, when people feel anxious walking through a dark parking lot at night, physical changes in the brain and body cause them to be alert and cautious of their surroundings. When students feel anxiety about an upcoming test, they may work harder to study and prepare for it. Without a little bit of anxiety, many students would be less motivated to study, write papers, or do homework. A small amount of anxiety boosts motivation and improves academic performance.

WHEN ANXIETY BECOMES A PROBLEM

While small amounts of anxiety are normal and sometimes even helpful, severe anxiety can become a serious issue. When anxiety becomes so intense that it begins to interfere with a person's daily life, the person may have an anxiety disorder. People with an anxiety disorder feel overwhelming worry and fear constantly. Instead of easing, anxiety does not go

THE HANDBOOK OF MENTAL DISORDERS

Mental health professionals across the United States and the world rely on the *Diagnostic and Statistical Manual of Mental Disorders, Fifth Edition* (*DSM-5*) to diagnose patients with anxiety and other mental health disorders. Published by the American Psychiatric Association, the *DSM-5* defines and classifies mental disorders in order to improve diagnoses. It contains descriptions, symptoms, and other criteria used to diagnose anxiety and other mental disorders. According to the *DSM-5*, anxiety disorders share characteristics of excessive fear and anxiety along with related behavioral disturbances. Anxiety disorders listed by the *DSM-5* include generalized anxiety disorder, separation anxiety disorder, selective mutism, specific phobia, social anxiety disorder, panic disorder, agoraphobia, substance-induced anxiety disorder, and anxiety disorders due to other medical conditions.

away and may even get worse over time. These extreme feelings of worry and fear can interfere with school, relationships with family and friends, and job performance.

Anxiety disorders are the most common mental health conditions in the United States. According to the National Alliance on Mental Illness (NAMI), more than 40 million adults in the United States have an anxiety disorder. In addition, about 7 percent of children between the ages of three and 17 experience problems with anxiety each year.[2] There are many types of anxiety disorders, including generalized anxiety disorder, social anxiety disorder, panic disorder, and specific phobias. Academic anxiety is not a separate diagnosis according to mental health experts but instead falls under the categories of generalized anxiety disorder or social anxiety disorder.

WHAT ACADEMIC ANXIETY LOOKS LIKE

For some students, anxiety grows so much that it affects their academic performance. They constantly worry about homework, tests, grades, and school projects. Over time, worrying thoughts prevent students from focusing on completing schoolwork successfully. The worrying thoughts become so intense students cannot stop thinking about future failure. They become preoccupied with worry about what will happen if they do poorly on a test or in a class. Becoming preoccupied with these worries can

Academic anxiety can cause physical symptoms, such as feeling light-headed.

lead students to think negatively about themselves and to doubt themselves and their abilities.

All of this worry often triggers physical symptoms in the body. Students may feel their heart beating faster or the palms of their hands becoming sweaty. Their muscles may tense, and their breathing rates may increase. They may feel nauseous or light-headed.

As students struggle with academic anxiety, they may start to engage in certain behaviors that make it

SUNEUNG IN SOUTH KOREA

College entrance exams are common in many countries. In South Korea, students who wish to go to college must take a series of tests called *Suneung*. Suneung is eight hours of back-to-back tests. Students' scores determine whether they can go to university and can affect their future job prospects and income. Because the pressure to do well is so intense, many Korean students begin preparing for the tests at as early as four years old. For Eun-suh, an 18-year-old student preparing to take the tests, a typical day of studying, school, and private tutoring begins at 7:30 a.m. and ends around midnight. With all of this academic pressure, Korean mental health experts worry about the burden on students' mental well-being. "They are growing up alone, just studying by themselves. This kind of isolation can cause depression and be a major factor in suicide," says Kim Tae-hyung, a Seoul-based psychologist.[3]

even more difficult to succeed at school. These behaviors can take many forms, but all cause more problems for the students. They can include difficulties preparing for tests, such as poor study habits or withdrawal from class activities. The problems can also affect test performance. For example, a student may feel extremely anxious when it is time to take a test. The student cannot shake the fear that she will run out of time or do poorly on the exam. During the test, her anxiety may drive her to constantly check the clock to see how much time is left. She may spend too much time trying to figure out a test question that she does not know. She may be too distracted by thoughts of failure to focus. As a result, she does not finish the test. Her anxious behaviors cause her fear of not finishing to become a reality, which in turn increases her anxiety.

Some students feel anxiety over every academic task. Others have specific anxiety related to math or taking tests. Rebecca Dillon, a teacher in Scotland, remembers that her anxiety over math emerged in high school. "As the difficulty of what I was learning increased to much more challenging concepts and areas of [math], my confidence in my own ability severely went downhill and all enjoyment I once felt for [math] was lost," she says. "Walking into the [math] classroom began to be the most daunting part of the day." After the teacher told Dillon she likely wouldn't pass the class, Dillon's anxiety worsened. "From that point on I was convinced I was completely unable

MALADAPTIVE PERFECTIONISM

Though many people are familiar with perfectionism, they might not know that there are different types of perfectionism. Adaptive perfectionism is setting high but realistic goals and putting in the effort to achieve those goals. An example could be a star swimmer on a school team aiming to beat his race time at every meet but accepting the results when he does not. Maladaptive perfectionism is the kind more often seen in cases of academic anxiety. Maladaptive perfectionism can hinder a person's ability to live a happy and successful life. Maladaptive perfectionists might have extremely negative attitudes when they don't achieve their goals, becoming self-critical and self-conscious. This can lead to avoidance of tasks due to fear of failure.

and therefore completely shut off and lost all concentration in the subject to avoid the distress it was bringing me," she says.[5] Eventually Dillon barely passed the class, but the anxiety caused her to give up studying advanced math.

CYCLE OF ACADEMIC ANXIETY

Students struggling with academic anxiety often find themselves in a destructive cycle of fear, negative thoughts, and unhelpful behaviors. They are so afraid of failing that they may not even try. Sarah Hanson is a licensed clinical social worker who works with preteens and teens. She says,

"Many students with academic anxiety are so fearful of falling short that they actually adopt the protective mindset of 'If I don't try, I can't fail.'"[6] The students convince themselves that they are not able to be successful on an assignment, so they end up not finishing it. They feel if they cannot complete a task perfectly, they should not complete it at all. This perfectionism can create more distress for students because they are failing to meet their own expectations. They also might feel like they are disappointing teachers and parents. It becomes an increasing cycle of fear and anxiety. In this way, academic anxiety can become more disruptive over time. Hanson says:

> *By not trying, the fear of failure actually compounds. When we don't face our fears—ultimately the fear increases and avoidance grows. I have worked with many students who have come to the point of rarely handing in assignments (especially writing) because an inner dialogue of doubt takes over: "What if I don't get a good grade?" "What if I am wrong?" "What if my teacher doesn't like it?" And though it defies logic, many students with a perfectionistic mindset would rather take a zero for a high-stakes assignment than risk passing in a less-than-stellar essay or project.[7]*

When goals of a dream school become conflated with a student's self-worth, rejection can be devastating.

MORGAN'S STORY

Morgan is a teen from New York who struggled throughout middle school and high school with academic anxiety. She felt immense pressure to be accepted to Columbia University, as five generations of her family had gone there, including her older brother. She says, "I hardly slept from the first day of sixth grade to the last day of high school, trying to achieve a 4.0 G.P.A. . . . The anxiety this caused me was not obvious—it was what I referred to as silent anxiety. I never felt right about complaining about how badly it was affecting me, because I had been given every opportunity to succeed and I shouldn't be complaining."[8]

During her senior year, Morgan found out that she was not accepted to Columbia. "I felt like my whole world had fallen apart. I felt like everything I had worked for was all a waste," she says. Yet years later, she realized that her denial from Columbia may have been the best thing to happen to her. For the first time in years, she felt free from the overwhelming pressure of school and grades. "I am now a sophomore at a college that I love and belong at," she says. "And though it took me almost 20 years to be rid of my anxiety, my rejection from my 'dream school' made me realize that we can't plan for forever and that there is nothing more important than today."[9]

Presenting in front of the class can cause anxiety for
some students.

CHAPTER THREE

SIGNS AND SYMPTOMS

Every student is different. This means the symptoms of academic anxiety can vary considerably. Symptoms can also range in severity. For some students, the symptoms of academic anxiety are mild, and the students are still able to perform fairly well in school. For others, symptoms are so severe they disrupt the students' daily lives and significantly affect their school performance. Academic anxiety can have both physical and emotional effects on its sufferers. "Test anxiety [and academic anxiety are] really a cognitive emotional and physical reaction to evaluation and the consequences of evaluation," says professor of school psychology Nathaniel von der Embse.[1]

PHYSICAL SYMPTOMS

Sometimes students dealing with academic anxiety experience physical symptoms. They may sweat, shake, or have rapid heartbeats. Their mouths may become dry, or they may develop headaches. They might experience gastrointestinal distress such as nausea or diarrhea. Some students become light-headed and feel as if they

RISING ENROLLMENT IN AP CLASSES

Across the United States, the number of students enrolled in Advanced Placement (AP) classes has been steadily rising. AP classes are specially designed courses that give high school students the experience of a college entry-level class and the potential to earn college credit while still in high school. Between 2009 and 2019, the number of public high school graduates who had taken at least one AP exam increased from 26 percent to 39 percent. The number of graduates who passed AP exams with a score of 3 or higher out of 5 also increased from 16 percent in 2009 to 24 percent in 2019. According to the College Board, the organization that administers AP exams, more than 1.2 million 2019 graduates took at least one AP exam across the United States.[3]

are going to faint. "I would always have trouble breathing when I was feeling anxious," says 15-year-old Annamarie, who is a straight-A student.[2]

Students with mild cases of academic anxiety may feel butterflies in their stomachs before a test or while working on an important assignment. For those with more severe anxiety, physical symptoms can cause a student to become ill and unable to function in her day-to-day life.

While sitting in her Advanced Placement (AP) English class, 17-year-old Salli-Ann Holloway could not breathe. Her body shook uncontrollably, and her neck twitched constantly. She gasped for air as her body went numb. As she had done many times before, Salli-Ann rushed to the school nurse's office. Physical symptoms like the ones she was experiencing had become a common occurrence for her as the stress of junior year gripped her. Salli-Ann says that the stress of AP and honors courses, along with a fear of the future, led to her anxiety. "A lot of people always say junior year is the hardest," she says. "With people telling me that, it got me in that mindset, and I was taking challenging classes. It was definitely a year when everybody did a lot of growing up and so a lot of things changed with your friendships, the classes and thinking about the future more than we've ever had to. That all just contributed and made it worse."[4]

SELF-HARM BEHAVIORS

Some people with an anxiety disorder experience the urge to self-harm. Not everyone with an anxiety disorder has this urge, but studies have linked self-harm and anxiety. People dealing with anxiety symptoms often feel overwhelmed and worried about situations they cannot control. For some people, self-harm behaviors such as cutting, scratching, burning, or hitting can provide relief from their anxious feelings. Other people engage in self-harm behaviors out of anger, because they are frustrated or mad that they cannot control their anxiety symptoms. While nonsuicidal self-injury disorder was not a separate mental health diagnosis in 2020, mental health experts have called for further study on the condition.

COGNITIVE AND BEHAVIORAL SYMPTOMS

Academic anxiety can also cause cognitive and behavioral symptoms. When anxious, students may have difficulty concentrating, and they might struggle with racing thoughts. Some students who are having trouble concentrating may appear to be daydreaming in class. "Some kids might appear really 'on' at one point but then they can suddenly drift away, depending on what they're feeling anxious about," says Ken Schuster, a neurologist and former teacher. "That looks like inattention, and it is, but it's triggered by anxiety." Some students find their minds seem to go blank and they forget what they already know during a test. That's because anxiety "tends to lock up the brain," Schuster says.[5] This can lead to negative self-talk, which is an inner conversation a person has with himself that limits his ability to believe in himself and his capabilities.

Students dealing with academic anxiety may also exhibit some behavioral symptoms, such as fidgeting, procrastinating, or avoiding tests or other academic situations. Schuster noted that anxious students avoided participating in class, even if they knew the material. Instead of raising their hands to answer questions, "They're going to break eye contact, they might look down, they might start writing something even though they're not really writing something. They're trying to break the connection with the teacher in order to avoid what's making them feel anxious," he says.[6] In some cases, the anxiety becomes so great that students begin to completely avoid situations that trigger fear. They avoid tests and may even begin to skip classes or school. Students might not turn in homework because they are worried it is not perfect. Academic anxiety can also lead

WHAT IS NEGATIVE SELF-TALK?

Everyone has a little voice inside that speaks up when he or she is about to make a bad choice. However, when this inner voice becomes excessively negative, it can create a significant amount of stress. Negative self-talk can tell people that they "are not good at math" or they "will never get into college." This negative inner dialogue can limit people's belief in themselves and hold them back from reaching their potential. Negative self-talk has also been linked to an increased risk of mental health problems. Over time, negative self-talk can decrease a person's motivation and increase feelings of stress and helplessness.

students to constantly redo work to meet a self-imposed standard of perfection. They end up spending so much time on an assignment that they never finish it. In some extreme cases, academic anxiety may become so severe that a student drops out of school entirely to avoid anxiety-inducing situations. Other students may turn to

Academic anxiety can lead to depression, panic attacks, and other distressing physical and emotional symptoms.

alcohol or drugs in an attempt to self-medicate and deal with their anxiety.

EMOTIONAL AND SOCIAL SYMPTOMS

The stress of academic anxiety on students can lead to emotional symptoms such as depression, anger, and low self-esteem. Poor grades and test scores reinforce students' negative thoughts and may cause them to blame themselves and feel worthless and inadequate compared to peers. Often, they feel helpless and unable to change the situation. This can also include social symptoms, such as a person withdrawing from her friends or becoming overly concerned about how her parents or teachers view her.

Amy Ebeling suffered from anxiety throughout her years at Ramapo College in New Jersey and experienced emotional highs and lows. "At my high points I was working several jobs and internships—I could take on the world," Ebeling said. "But then I would have extreme downs and want to do nothing. All I wanted to do was sleep. I screwed up in school and at work, I was crying and feeling suicidal." During her senior year, Ebeling reached her breaking point. "I thought that it was a weakness—'why can't I just snap out of it?' . . . It became apparent it just wasn't that easy. . . . In one class I panicked so much, I freaked out. I dragged myself to the counseling center," she said.[7]

WHEN PANIC STRIKES

In some cases, academic anxiety can trigger panic attacks. A panic attack is a surge of intense fear or discomfort during which a person experiences physical symptoms such as a pounding heart, chest pain, or fear of dying. These physical symptoms can be so intense that sufferers

THE PROBLEM WITH PROCRASTINATION

Procrastination is the practice of putting off something that needs to be done. Procrastinating on schoolwork or studying is a component of academic anxiety. The longer students procrastinate, the more rushed they feel about completing an assignment or studying for a test. In turn, this can lead to an increase in anxiety, stress, and fear about school. These feelings, along with a fear of disapproval from parents and teachers, can lead to even more procrastination.

mistake panic attacks for heart attacks.

Marcia Morris is a psychiatrist at the University of Florida with more than 20 years of experience providing clinical care for students. Morris said:

> One of the most anxious students I treated was Jen, a pre-medical student in her sophomore year. Her mother encouraged her to see a psychiatrist, and even went with her to the first appointment. Jen was shaking. She said she was so anxious that it hurt. She was having at least one panic attack per day. It would start when she struggled with a difficult homework assignment. Her heart raced, her chest hurt, she felt like throwing up, and she started to sweat. Last week she went to the emergency room thinking she was having a heart attack.[9]

DIAGNOSING ACADEMIC ANXIETY

While it is normal to feel anxious from time to time, if anxiety symptoms are severe and last for several weeks, it may be time to seek help. "When your mood state interferes with your ability to function at school, like when you're finding you can't get to class, and you don't want to hang out with your friends or teammates, and you're having difficulty concentrating because you're feeling so distressed—that's when we want to . . . help you," says Dori Hutchinson, director of services at Boston University's Center for Psychiatric Rehabilitation.[10]

Academic anxiety can linger for weeks, months, or years. As time passes, anxiety symptoms often grow worse if left untreated. "The quicker you deal with it the better," says Debra Kissen, clinical director at an anxiety treatment center. "Or it can become

"WE SEE NORMAL ANXIETY MORPH INTO DISTRESS WHEN A STUDENT IS HAVING PANIC ATTACKS, CAN'T SLEEP OR SLOW THEMSELVES DOWN, PERSISTENTLY WORRIES OR OBSESSES ABOUT WHAT'S NEXT, OR IS HAVING OTHER PHYSICAL SYMPTOMS CONSISTENT WITH ANXIETY."[11]

—CARRIE LANDA, DIRECTOR OF BEHAVIORAL MEDICINE AT BOSTON UNIVERSITY'S STUDENT HEALTH SERVICES years of 'Oh, I don't want to take that test so I'm going to take a different major, now I'm not happy and I feel unsatisfied, and I feel like a loser because I don't have a career I believe in and now I'm depressed and it's impacting my relationships,' and so on. The longer it goes on the more it starts impacting other things."[12]

A doctor or mental health professional can diagnose a patient with an anxiety disorder. Because academic anxiety is not a specific mental health disorder, often a person will be diagnosed with generalized anxiety disorder or social anxiety disorder. At the first appointment, the doctor or mental health professional will ask the patient detailed questions in order to evaluate the patient's condition.

SELECTIVE MUTISM

Selective mutism is an anxiety disorder. It occurs when a person experiences a persistent failure to speak in certain social situations, even if the person can speak normally in more familiar settings. Parents often notice selective mutism in children before the age of five, but it is often not diagnosed until a child starts attending school and the symptoms become more noticeable. For example, a child with selective mutism may speak normally at home with family but not speak at school. The child may spend an entire school year without talking once to classmates, teachers, or counselors. In this way, selective mutism can interfere with students' academic performance at school as well as their social interactions.

To be diagnosed with an anxiety disorder, a person must visit a doctor or mental health professional.

Psychological questionnaires record a patient's feelings, physical symptoms, and daily experiences and can help with diagnoses. The mental health professional will also ask about the patient's medical and psychological history.

During the evaluation, mental health professionals will do a physical exam and look for any medications, illnesses, or physical conditions that may be causing anxiety symptoms. They may order blood or urine tests if they suspect a medical condition exists. If they determine that the patient has an anxiety disorder, they will work with the patient to develop an appropriate treatment plan.

Having a parent with anxiety or witnessing a trauma are both risk factors for developing anxiety.

CHAPTER FOUR

CAUSES OF ACADEMIC ANXIETY

While no one knows the exact cause of academic anxiety, mental health professionals believe a combination of several factors contributes to the risk of developing academic anxiety. These factors can be physical, genetic, or environmental. Because every person reacts differently to the same factors, it is often difficult to predict who will develop an anxiety disorder. And because there are so many possible causes of academic anxiety, every person's solution will be different.

PHYSICAL CAUSES

Certain physical conditions can increase a person's risk of developing an anxiety disorder, according to the National Institute of Mental Health (NIMH). In some cases, anxiety symptoms are the first signs of an underlying medical illness. If a doctor suspects that a patient's anxiety is related to a medical cause, the doctor may order tests to find the problem. Conditions such as heart disease, diabetes, respiratory disorders, thyroid disorders, irritable bowel syndrome (IBS), or chronic pain may cause anxiety symptoms. In addition, consuming caffeine or other substances, including some medications, can produce anxiety symptoms or make them worse.

Mental health professionals believe imbalances in brain chemistry may also increase a person's likelihood of developing all types of anxiety, including academic anxiety. Researchers believe that people who struggle with anxiety may experience excessive activation of the brain mechanism that controls fear and the body's fight-or-flight response. For example, the amygdala is a structure in the brain's limbic system that sends a warning when danger is present. It sends a message to another brain structure, the hypothalamus, which prompts the quick release of hormones that prepare the body to fight or flee by raising heart rate and blood pressure and tensing muscles. In a person with an anxiety disorder, the amygdala may be extremely sensitive, and it may overreact to events and situations that are not truly threatening, triggering the brain and body's danger response. Because the amygdala also has a role in storing emotional memories, anxiety can become linked over time to thoughts and situations that are not truly dangerous, such as a test or school assignment.

GENES, ENVIRONMENT, AND STRESS

People of all ages, races, and social statuses develop anxiety disorders. Certain groups of people, however, tend to experience anxiety disorders more often

BUILDING RESILIENCE

Some educators and mental health experts believe building resilience in today's youth can help students better cope with academic anxiety and other mental health disorders. A person with resilience is able to mentally and emotionally deal with a crisis to quickly return to precrisis status. Today, many youths have few opportunities to practice and build resilience, according to licensed mental health counselor and educator Josephine Kim. They have little practice making mistakes and recovering from them. Particularly in wealthy communities, parents are often very involved in their children's academic and social lives. It has become common for teens to study, meet with teachers about a bad grade, talk to coaches, and resolve disagreements with friends all with their parents' help. To help students build resilience, parents and teachers can help them learn to make positive social connections, build self-confidence through helping others, learn self-care, and set reasonable goals and make plans to work toward them.

than others. Research has shown that people are more likely to develop an anxiety disorder, including academic anxiety, if they have a close relative who has an anxiety disorder or other type of mental disorder, according to NIMH. A 2017 review of several clinical studies found that generalized anxiety disorder can be inherited and is linked to a number of different genes.[2]

Environmental factors can also increase a person's risk of developing many types of anxiety, including academic anxiety. Children who experience or witness abuse or trauma have an increased risk of developing an anxiety disorder. Stress is another factor that can increase this risk. Stress can be related to a major event, such as a death in the family, a serious illness, or financial problems

PERSONALITY

A person's personality may be another factor in whether the person suffers from anxiety. According to Harvard University psychologist Jerome Kagan, decades of study have shown that children who are shy have a higher risk of developing anxiety as they grow older. Research suggests the link between shyness and anxiety may be explained by certain physiological traits common in shy people. For example, shy children often have heightened excitability of the amygdala, a structure in the brain that signals when danger is near. People with certain anxiety disorders also have an overly sensitive amygdala. Researchers suspect that this trait may make a person more vulnerable to anxiety.

at home. Smaller stresses can also build up over time and trigger excessive anxiety.

HIGH EXPECTATIONS CREATE STRESS

In the case of academic anxiety, stress is often caused by high expectations in school. Students may face a lot of pressure to take the hardest classes while also juggling a variety of extracurricular activities in order to build a good résumé for college and beyond. Many teens spend hours in class and at home studying while also trying to manage a full calendar of sports practices and games, volunteering, part-time jobs, and other activities. "So now, everyone is taking the hardest classes, but it's not just grades, because they're told they not only have to be involved in clubs and sports, but they need to be the leader or captain. And they also need a high test score on the ACT and SAT," says Tom Koulentes, principal of Libertyville High School in Illinois.

"I've had conversations with former students who have told me, 'College is actually easier than high school.' In high school, they're dealing with hard, hard classes, and then they have three, four, or more hours of homework each night."[4]

The pressure to succeed in school and the high expectations placed upon students by themselves and their families can cause significant stress. Beth Sosler, who tutors high school students in Illinois, has noticed an increase in school-related stress and anxiety in teens. "We've seen more and more students with diagnosed or undiagnosed anxiety," Sosler says. "We are seeing more and more students being tutored for classes they are not ready for, but feel the pressure to be in. . . . What is happening is, you have students who are in over their heads. They are stressed to death."[5]

According to Noah Brookhim, a senior at Millburn High School in New Jersey, overloaded AP schedules are costing students precious hours of sleep. His classmates say they regularly get only four or five hours of rest at night. "Many students may feel compelled to take multiple AP or accelerated courses in order to make their transcripts more appealing to colleges. As a result, they're not able to maintain a healthy balance between schoolwork and their lives outside of school," Brookhim says.[6]

In addition to academic work, many students are involved in extracurricular activities.

ACADEMIC ANXIETY AND ADHD

While anyone can develop academic anxiety, students who already have attention deficit hyperactivity disorder (ADHD) may have an elevated risk for anxiety symptoms. ADHD is a neurodevelopmental disorder that can cause difficulty paying attention, impulsive behaviors, and heightened activity levels. Students with ADHD often find

People with ADHD can find it hard to focus in class.

it difficult to focus and pay attention in school, which can trigger anxiety. As students get older and schoolwork becomes more difficult, their anxiety symptoms often increase. Problems with skills such as paying attention or being organized can lead to missed assignments or not managing time well enough to finish projects and homework. As they struggle and fall behind, students experience more stress and anxiety.

To cope, some students choose to focus on a single important assignment or a single class and leave other schoolwork undone. Some even choose to avoid schoolwork entirely. However, these choices typically lead to even more anxiety, negative thoughts, and self-doubt.

ACADEMIC ANXIETY AND GIFTED CHILDREN

While many factors play roles in who develops academic anxiety, some characteristics of gifted children, commonly defined as children who are capable of high achievement in intellectual, creative, artistic, academic, or leadership areas, may make them more susceptible. Many gifted children are perfectionists, particularly in academic or extracurricular activities. They often develop unrealistically high expectations of

WHO IS A "GIFTED" STUDENT?

In the early 1920s, a psychologist named Lewis Terman advocated for schools to use intelligence quotient (IQ) tests to identify gifted students who were capable of high academic achievement. Students who scored 135 or higher on the IQ test were considered gifted. In the early 1970s, the definition of *gifted* was broadened to its current definition. Today, many schools in the United States still use Terman's classification system and IQ testing to identify gifted students.

themselves, especially if they typically do well in these areas. They may become unusually focused on finishing assignments without a mistake or become extremely frustrated with less-than-perfect grades. "Gifted kids tend to be perfectionists," explains Dan Peters, a psychologist who treats children with anxiety and other mental illnesses. "They feel they should perform and achieve at the highest possible levels in everything and fear making mistakes and failing. Thus, they often avoid doing things they don't think they can [do] 'perfectly,' and fear new things."[7] When gifted students are unable to meet their own lofty standards, their perfectionism may lead to academic anxiety and the fear of failure. Parents and teachers may unknowingly feed a gifted student's perfectionism by telling him they expect superior work from him.

Research has found that gifted students tend to experience high levels of empathy and are more sensitive, which allows them to better feel what others around them are feeling. As a result, they are very aware of disapproval or lack of approval from parents or teachers. They may feel responsible when disapproval relates to school performance, which can become a source of stress and lead to feelings of anxiety.

While gifted students may excel in certain areas, they may not excel in others. For example, students may excel at math but struggle with writing. This uneven development

Gifted students can struggle with perfectionism and
high expectations.

may cause students to become frustrated and confused,
especially if they have set high expectations for
themselves. This can increase self-doubt and self-criticism,
both of which can lead to an increase in anxiety.

Paula Prober is a psychotherapist who specializes in
dealing with gifted adults and children. One of her clients,
16-year-old Ben, struggled in school with anxiety. As a
young child, learning came easily to Ben. He could read and

People who naturally excel in the classroom may not have developed the study skills to handle more difficult material.

remember everything. When he started school, he already knew the material. The problem for Ben, however, was that he had started to believe that all learning should be easy. When school became hard, Ben did not know how to handle it, and he began to experience anxiety symptoms. Prober said:

> Ben never learned how to study. Or that it was normal for some learning to be a struggle. Ironically, even though he felt like a failure and like he wasn't smart because of his experiences in school, he also

believed that he shouldn't have to study something to understand it. This created confusion, anxiety, paralysis, and avoidance when there was a chance that he might not grasp a concept fast enough or succeed at a task. If it wasn't easy, he didn't do it.[8]

Anxiety is not always easy to identify and treat because it is not caused by a single factor. Instead, a combination of physical, genetic, and environmental factors contribute to the development of academic anxiety. Every person responds differently to anxiety's risk factors. A combination of factors may lead to anxiety in one person while another person with the same risk factors will not experience anxiety. Although it is difficult to predict who will develop an anxiety disorder, understanding risk factors can help a person be more aware of potential warning signs and make life changes to reduce the risks.

Academic anxiety can have a variety of negative effects on teens' lives.

EFFECTS ON DAILY LIFE

Academic anxiety, like many forms of anxiety, can affect a person's life in a variety of ways. It can negatively affect a student's performance in school. Academic anxiety can also cause people to feel bad about themselves, lowering self-esteem and confidence. It can trigger physical problems such as headaches or digestive problems. As academic anxiety worsens over time, it can lead to other mental health disorders, such as depression and other forms of anxiety.

EFFECT ON ACADEMIC PERFORMANCE

While a little bit of anxiety can help student performance, when anxiety is severe, it can have a negative effect instead. One reason may be the way in which anxiety interferes with the brain's working memory. Working memory holds pieces of information while people actively think about them. Working memory helps a person solve problems effectively and manage information in the current moment. Research has shown that when people experience high levels of anxiety, their ability

WHAT IS WORKING MEMORY?

Working memory is the brain's ability to hold new information so a person can then use it. Students rely on working memory in school. For example, a teacher asks a student to add 15 and 13 in his head and then subtract four. Working memory allows the student to remember the numbers long enough to perform the calculations. The student may not remember the numbers by his next class, but working memory has done its job and allowed the student to successfully complete the short-term task. Working memory holds new information briefly so that the brain can work with it. It also helps the brain organize new information and send it elsewhere for long-term memory storage.

to hold information in working memory suffers. When working memory is not operating at normal levels, a person may have trouble concentrating and may make more mistakes. It may also be more difficult to complete tasks efficiently. As a result, students with high levels of academic anxiety may find it more difficult to remember information they studied or to focus on tests and assignments, which causes their academic performance to suffer. "When students are anxious, their worries use up some of their working memory, leaving fewer cognitive resources to devote to the test," says cognitive scientist Sian Beilock.[1]

College students report that anxiety and stress are the two greatest factors affecting their academic performance,

according to the 2019 National College Health Assessment
by the American College Health Association. Nearly
28 percent of students surveyed named anxiety as a factor
causing an academic
impact, while 34 percent
named stress as a
factor.[2] In the survey,
academic impact was
defined as receiving a
lower grade on a test,
on a project, or in a
course; receiving an
incomplete or dropping a
course; or experiencing a
significant disruption in
research or thesis work.

    Emmanuel
Mennesson began to
experience symptoms
of anxiety as a freshman
studying engineering

EXECUTIVE FUNCTION

Research has linked anxiety
disorders with problems in
executive functioning. The
brain's executive function is often
described as its management
system. It controls working
memory, flexible thinking, and
self-control. The brain's executive
function is responsible for several
skills that are important for
students. These include paying
attention, organizing, planning,
prioritizing, staying focused until
tasks are completed, regulating
emotions, and monitoring the
self. These skills develop through
early childhood and into the
teenage years.

at McGill University in Montreal, Canada. He quickly
became overwhelmed with his classes and workload and
felt lost in classes with hundreds of students. He began
skipping classes and not turning in assignments. "I was
totally ashamed of what happened. I didn't want to let my

parents down, so I retreated inward," he said.[3] In his second semester of freshman year, Mennesson did not go to a single class. That April, he withdrew from college.

LOWER SELF-ESTEEM

Like many forms of anxiety, academic anxiety can affect the way people see themselves. For many students, their self-image and self-esteem are linked to their academic performance. When they do not perform as well as they had hoped, they may bombard themselves with negative thoughts, such as "I'm such an idiot" or "I'll never be successful." These self-criticizing thoughts are common and become worse in stressful situations, such as working on a major project or taking an important test. Frequent negative thinking can damage a person's self-esteem. The more negative thinking a person experiences, the more likely it is that his self-esteem and his view of himself will suffer.

Bad grades can lower a student's self-esteem, which can in turn make academic anxiety worse.

As a student's self-esteem drops, her academic performance can further suffer in a vicious cycle. "A student's self-esteem has a significant impact on almost everything she does—on the way she engages in activities, deals with challenges, and interacts with others. Self-esteem also can have a marked effect on academic performance. Low self-esteem can lessen a student's desire to learn, her ability to focus, and her willingness to take risks," says Kenneth Shore, a psychologist for the Hamilton, New Jersey, public schools.[5]

PHYSICAL EFFECTS

Academic anxiety affects more than the mind; it also affects people physically. For people with academic anxiety, changes in appetite and sleep patterns, headaches, and gastrointestinal (GI) distress are common. "From head to toe, almost every system can be impacted just by nature of your body releasing a lot of stress hormones," says Mona Potter, medical director at McLean Anxiety Mastery Program in Boston, Massachusetts.[6]

How anxiety affects each person physically varies. Some people might have trouble falling asleep or staying asleep as elevated levels of hormones such as adrenaline and cortisol make it difficult for the body to relax.

IMPACT ON RELATIONSHIPS

Generalized anxiety disorder, which can include academic anxiety, can negatively affect a person's relationships with family and friends. Some people find themselves becoming overly dependent on a friend, family member, or partner. They rely on this person constantly for support and seek out constant reassurance. If a friend does not respond immediately, the person may get anxious. Other people with generalized anxiety disorder push away friends and family. They decide to avoid close relationships so that they do not have to talk about their feelings, become vulnerable, or risk disappointing other people.

Anxiety can have a particularly strong effect on the gastrointestinal system, causing stomachaches and digestion problems.

Racing thoughts that come with anxiety can also disturb sleep and make it difficult to feel calm. Other people may experience stomachaches, constipation, or other gastrointestinal problems. "Anxiety really hits the GI system hard," Potter says.[7]

Haley Tiffany is a teen struggling with anxiety at school. She says, "Every day is a challenge. I wake up with a nervous stomachache. I get dressed and put on my mascara, trying to hold the brush tightly with shaky hands. I try to eat something, but I can't. Everything makes me feel sick. At school I greet my friends with a fake smile and try to appear as calm as can be." In class, Haley finds it difficult to focus and pay attention to the teacher. She says:

In class I change my position many times in my desk. I cannot sit still. My mind wanders off into so many places. . . . I sketch flowers with vines along the margin. I shouldn't be doodling in class at my age, but I can't help it. I drop my pen. My hands are shaking. Now my legs are shaking. I can't breathe. I feel dizzy, and my head is swaying from side to side. My desk is shaking now. My whole body is shaking. . . . The teacher is at the front of the room. I'm in the back, suffocating.[8]

OTHER MENTAL HEALTH ISSUES

Over time, severe academic anxiety can lead to other mental health issues. While depression and anxiety are different conditions, they often occur together. Depression is a mental disorder that involves debilitating sadness that interferes with a person's ability to participate in daily life. For some people, anxiety is a symptom of clinical depression, as people who are depressed often worry and feel anxious. For others, anxiety can be a trigger for depression. In fact, the chance of developing depression is much higher for those who already have an anxiety disorder. "It's a cycle," says Sally R. Connolly, a licensed clinical social worker and therapist. "When you get anxious, you tend to have this pervasive thinking about some worry or some problem. You feel bad about it. Then you feel like you've failed. You move to depression."[10] When anxiety and depression occur together, the symptoms can become more severe than when each disorder occurs by itself. In addition, when a person has both anxiety and depression, both disorders are more difficult to treat.

SUBSTANCE ABUSE

To cope with anxiety symptoms, some people turn to alcohol or drugs to self-medicate and avoid dealing with their symptoms. According to the National Institute on Drug Abuse (NIDA), people with anxiety are two times more likely to suffer from substance abuse problems than those who do not have an anxiety disorder.[11] Instead of helping, however, alcohol and drugs often intensify and worsen a person's anxiety symptoms. This can create a cycle of substance abuse, which can lead to addiction.

People having suicidal thoughts should seek the help of a trusted adult. The number of the National Suicide Prevention Lifeline is 1-800-273-TALK (8255).

For some students, the pressures of academic anxiety can become so intense that they think about suicide. When Taylor Chiu was a high school freshman in 2002, she attempted suicide to escape the constant academic pressure she felt. Chiu's schedule was packed with schoolwork, swim team practices, band practices, and Girl Scout meetings. She often left her house in the morning when it was still dark and did not return until night. The constant pressure to keep up her grades and juggle activities quickly became too much. "I was exhausted to the bone," she says. "I remember just not being happy about anything, and I just couldn't make it slow down. And I thought there would never be any escape." She felt traumatized when she got an F on a geometry test. She began to dread swim practices and other activities that she used to enjoy. "I also felt like I was already saying that I was too stressed, and nobody—neither my parents nor my teachers—seemed to care or take me seriously," she says. Then one night Chiu purposely took too many ibuprofen pills. "The only reason I waffled was because I knew it would probably break my mom's heart, and I didn't know if I could do that to her," Chiu says. A little while later, when her younger brother noticed she was acting strangely, Chiu confessed that she'd swallowed the pills. Her parents drove her to the hospital, where Chiu was treated. Today, she feels lucky that she survived.[12]

When allowed to grow, academic anxiety can affect nearly every part of a person's life. The consuming fear and worry caused by academic anxiety can quickly disrupt a person's physical well-being, sleep, and diet. Left unchecked, it can also affect self-esteem, mental health, academic performance, and more. But there are many ways to fight back.

With treatment, academic anxiety can be reduced and sometimes eliminated.

CHAPTER SIX

OVERCOMING ACADEMIC ANXIETY

Like other illnesses, anxiety disorders can be treated. Once a person has been diagnosed with an anxiety disorder by a mental health professional, the patient can work with the doctor to develop a treatment plan. Some people with milder symptoms can overcome anxiety with lifestyle changes. Others who have more intense symptoms may respond better to psychotherapy, medication, or a combination of the two. "The most important thing is often the hardest and that's just getting help. Anxiety is probably the most common mental health illness and the least taboo," says Quinita Ellis, a licensed mental health counselor. "My advice to high school students is to decide. Decide if this is something that you feel like you can manage on your own or do you need help? If you have tried to manage this on your own and you know that it's causing some type of dysfunction in your relationships or in school, you probably need professional help."[1]

PSYCHOTHERAPY

Psychotherapy is a common treatment for anxiety disorders. During a psychotherapy session, patients talk to a mental health professional about their feelings and problems and learn about ways to deal with them. Effective psychotherapy focuses on a person's specific anxieties and needs. It can take place in individual, group, or family sessions.

One of the most common types of psychotherapy used to help people with anxiety disorders is cognitive behavioral therapy (CBT). CBT is based on the idea that people's thoughts influence their feelings and behaviors, and that negative thoughts about a situation will lead to negative feelings and behaviors. Therefore, the goal of CBT is to teach people different ways of thinking, behaving, and reacting to situations and things that produce anxiety and fear. In regular meetings

"IT WAS ONLY WHEN I VOICED MY EMOTIONS TO MY ADVISER THAT I BEGAN TO FEEL LESS ALONE. I STILL FEEL THE ANXIETY CREEPING IN BEFORE EXAMS, WHEN THE FAMILIAR SUFFOCATING FEELING RETURNS, AND I HAVE TO REMIND MYSELF THAT MY ENTIRE FUTURE IS NOT DEPENDENT ON ONE EXAM."[2]

—SARAH, A COLLEGE STUDENT FROM RHODE ISLAND

Group therapy can introduce patients to others who are going through the same struggles.

with a trained and licensed CBT therapist, patients work to identify, understand, and change their thinking and behavior patterns related to anxiety.

Exposure therapy is a CBT method sometimes used to treat people with anxiety. Exposure therapy focuses on confronting the underlying fears driving a person's anxiety. During exposure therapy, the patient is gradually exposed to situations that trigger fear in a safe, controlled environment. Mental health professionals often begin by having a patient repeatedly imagine a feared situation or object and her response to it. Some professionals may incorporate virtual reality or computer simulations as safe methods of exposure therapy. A mental health professional

HYPNOTHERAPY

While many people know about hypnotism from pop culture and movies, hypnotherapy may also be used to reduce anxiety symptoms. Hypnotherapy helps patients use breathing, guided imagery, or muscle-relaxing techniques to fall into a very relaxed state. In this state, the patient is more receptive to suggestions. Hypnotherapists can use imagery or simple verbal suggestions to lessen anxiety symptoms. For some patients, hypnotherapy can provide relief from symptoms after only a few sessions. If the therapy shows positive results, the hypnotherapist may also teach the patient ways to perform self-hypnosis to manage anxiety symptoms.

may ask a student to write a paragraph with grammatical errors or a disorganized construction. While this can be very uncomfortable for a person with perfectionist characteristics, it can also be very powerful by showing him that he can handle it when something goes wrong. The repeated exposure to feared situations in a safe environment can help reduce a patient's fear and anxiety. "If you move toward the thing that makes you anxious, your confidence goes up and your anxiety goes down," says Scott Bea, a psychologist with the Cleveland Clinic.[3]

MEDICATION

For teens with moderate to severe anxiety, medication may be necessary to manage the illness. One example is antidepressants, which are medications used to treat depression. Some can also be used to treat anxiety. Selective serotonin reuptake inhibitors (SSRIs) are antidepressants commonly prescribed for anxiety in children and teens. These medications work by increasing levels of the neurotransmitter serotonin in the brain by blocking it from being reabsorbed by the brain's nerve cells. With more serotonin available, mood improves.

Another class of antidepressants called serotonin-norepinephrine reuptake inhibitors (SNRIs) can also be prescribed for teens with anxiety. SNRIs block the reabsorption of the neurotransmitters serotonin and norepinephrine in

STIGMA OF MEDICATION

Not everyone who has a mental disorder needs to take medication. However, those who do may hesitate to get the help they need because of a stigma toward medication. *Stigma* refers to negative and often unfair beliefs that a society or group of people has about something. Some people believe that those who take medication for mental illnesses are not trying hard enough to overcome the disorders. They may also believe a person simply needs to eat a certain diet, exercise, or meditate to cure depression and anxiety. Unfortunately, these attitudes can prevent patients from seeking treatment and taking medication that could help them. In recent years, however, open discussions by celebrities, athletes, and other well-known personalities about their battles with depression, anxiety, and other mental health disorders have helped make it easier to talk about mental illness and treatment options, including medication.

the brain. Some teens who take SSRIs or SNRIs for anxiety experience side effects, including dizziness, dry mouth, excessive sweating, headache, and nausea. Most of the time, these side effects are mild and disappear within a few weeks.

For teens with social anxiety and phobias, a doctor may prescribe a medication called a beta-blocker. This type of medication relieves a teen's physical symptoms such as sweating, shaking, and heart palpitations. Beta-blockers can cause some side effects including headaches, nausea, constipation, and cold hands.

While doctors may prescribe benzodiazepines such as Klonopin for adults with anxiety, this type of medication is generally not prescribed for teens. Benzodiazepines can be addictive and can cause powerful withdrawal symptoms. In addition, there is little scientific evidence that this type of medication is effective in treating anxiety in children and teens.

Medication affects every person differently. It may take some time for a patient and her doctor to find the most effective medication and dosage. A patient should be careful to take her medication only as prescribed in order to improve effectiveness and reduce side effects. In some cases, a patient may decide to stop taking her medication because of its side effects. However, a patient should

Doctors can determine whether medication is the right form of treatment for someone with anxiety.

always discuss this decision with her doctor so they can determine the safest way to taper off medication.

SUPPORT AT SCHOOL

As anxiety rises among teens, schools are increasingly focusing on student mental health needs and developing ways to best support anxious students. In many schools, school counselors are teaching students how to cope with and overcome anxiety, rather than just avoid the people and situations that make them anxious. Until students learn how to cope with academic stress and feelings of discomfort and panic, their problems with anxiety will only continue.

While the approach for supporting each student is unique, "The first step is usually to get the student back into class, comfortable, and able to learn," says Beth O'Brien, an adjustment counselor at Newton North High School in Massachusetts. "And counselors need to give students . . . the tools to do that."[4] According to O'Brien, school counselors can begin by determining what situations, activities, or objects make a student anxious. The counselor and student can then brainstorm ways to make the situation or activity less fearful and more manageable. For example, if a student becomes anxious in chemistry class, the counselor may suggest the student move his seat or talk to the teacher. These actions give the student some control over the situation, which can build resilience.

In regular counseling sessions, school counselors can also help students practice strategies to calm themselves and refocus thoughts when they feel anxiety rising. "Many students with anxiety want to avoid their trigger, but counselors should expose students to what they're fearful of, in a healthy way that won't induce more panic," says O'Brien.[5]

Schools and counselors can also provide certain accommodations for students diagnosed with anxiety.

A school counselor can help a student come up with ways to manage her academic anxiety.

Some schools have created safe, quiet spaces where students can retreat when feeling anxious and overwhelmed. Students may also be given extra time for tests or be allowed to take tests in a separate, quiet environment. Students who get anxious standing up in front of the class may be allowed to record their presentations or only give them to the teacher. They may receive modified tests and homework. To prevent large assignments from becoming overwhelming, the teacher may break them down into smaller, more manageable pieces. Students may receive preferential seating in class and be allowed to record lectures. Some schools also assign students a

LACK OF MENTAL HEALTH SERVICES IN SCHOOLS

Despite the rise in mental health concerns for students, many school districts lack qualified mental health professionals to deal with them. As schools face budget pressures, many districts have cut or not filled positions for school psychologists. Not having these mental health professionals in schools significantly limits the schools' abilities to address students' mental health issues. School guidance counselors are often tapped to fill the role. While guidance counselors have training to guide students through social and emotional issues, their services are often short-term and responsive to specific events rather than long-term. As a result, many students lack the mental health help that they desperately need.

specific adult at school, often a counselor, to go to when feeling anxious or overwhelmed.

In high-achieving schools, the pressure to succeed can be extreme. Counselors can step in and speak up for students, encouraging them not to overload themselves academically. Counselors may suggest students take fewer AP or honors classes and encourage them to participate in extracurricular activities they enjoy and that make them feel good about themselves, which can offset the stress of intense academic pressure. Counselors can also work with teachers to help their students learn how to manage stress, embrace challenges, accept mistakes, and handle feeling overwhelmed. "Educators who take this approach offer positive encouragement that reinforces effort, as well as helpful instructional feedback on learning strategies," says clinical psychologist Jacqueline Zeller. "Helping students to have freedom to feel mistakes are part of the learning process will allow for students to focus more on developing effective strategies connected to the academic task at hand, rather than worrying about getting a perfect score on a test."[6]

POSITIVE STUDY HABITS

In many cases, students with academic anxiety find that improving their study skills can make them feel more confident and can reduce feelings of anxiety. Successful students are prepared. They learn good note-taking skills in a way that works for them. Some students prefer handwritten notes, some take notes on a laptop or tablet when permitted by teachers, and others make an audio recording of a lecture and write notes later. They organize their notes so they do not waste time trying to find them when studying for a test. To minimize anxiety, students can also develop study strategies that use their learning styles. Some students learn best by listening, some learn by doing, and others find that reading and writing helps them learn material most effectively.

Developing good study habits can help students overcome academic anxiety.

Time management is another essential skill for reducing academic anxiety. Students who effectively manage their time create flexible study schedules and task lists. They stick to their schedules and find strategies to avoid procrastinating and putting off studying or working on assignments. By doing so, they are able to avoid a considerable amount of stress caused by completing assignments at the last minute or losing sleep by studying all night before a test. Students can also schedule personal time to relax and reduce stress. "I have a daily planner, but I also use a chalkboard wall, sticky notes, and an app on my phone to make reminders and notes of encouragement more visible. It's one of the best things I've done to cope with both anxiety and ADHD," says Kami L., a young woman who struggles with academic anxiety.[7]

Often, academic anxiety results from high expectations and sometimes unrealistic goals that students set for themselves. The anxiety becomes counterproductive and can make it more difficult for students to achieve their goals. Sometimes lowering goals can have the effect of improving a student's performance. If students do not put pressure on themselves to score an A on a test, they may feel less anxious when taking it. As a result, they may be able to focus more and better remember the material they studied. Instead of setting a goal to have the highest grade, students may be better off striving to feel good about their performance and preparation. Often, students find that working through these issues with a trained mental health counselor can help them stop holding themselves to unrealistic goals and expectations.

KEEPING CALM

If students feel worry and fear building, several relaxation techniques can help them remain calm. Deep breathing or tensing and relaxing different muscle groups helps to focus a student's attention on something other than fears. Some students find using guided imagery reduces anxiety.

With guided imagery, a person envisions a scene that he finds peaceful and relaxing. He focuses on what he hears, sees, feels, and smells while in this scene.

Positive self-talk can also reduce anxiety in the classroom or at home. Students think about helpful responses to counter the negative thoughts that come with anxiety. For example, instead of thinking that they are going to fail the test, they tell themselves that they have prepared well and can handle it. They acknowledge their anxiety and tell themselves that a little bit of nervousness can help them do their best. Instead of becoming overwhelmed by a large assignment, they focus on breaking it down into smaller pieces.

IT CAN GET BETTER

With the right treatment, academic anxiety can get better. When Victoria Pae was a freshman at Boston University majoring in neuroscience and psychology, she felt overwhelmed with stress and anxiety. "Everyone was doing so much, everyone was so on top of their games, it seemed like they had it all together," says Pae. "You're seeing everyone excelling above you. And even though you have the ability to excel too, you're too scared of making a fool of yourself to actually try to do it."[9]

Pae was reluctant to admit she had a problem and to seek help. Instead, she hid her feelings of anxiety. "I didn't want to tell myself that I needed to get help, so I didn't," she says. "I just told myself, it's all in my head, get over it."[10] Eventually, her grades began to suffer, and she sought help from a therapist.

With treatment, Pae became better equipped to handle her anxiety. "I won't say I'm 100 percent OK now, as I still have my moments of self-doubt and of neglecting self-care, but I'm definitely doing better than I was a couple of years ago," she says. Her experience has helped her realize the benefits of getting help for anxiety. "I think a lot of students . . . are scared to admit that they're stressed and worried their life might be crumbling before their eyes," she says. She advises students that "whether the difficulties you're going through are major or minor, it's OK to seek help."[11]

Exercise is one of many lifestyle changes that can help people manage anxiety.

CHAPTER SEVEN

LIVING WITH LESS STRESS

Treatment for anxiety can greatly reduce and even eliminate anxiety symptoms and improve quality of life. In addition, people who suffer from anxiety, including academic anxiety, have found that making a few lifestyle changes and adopting healthy habits can help ease their anxiety symptoms.

REGULAR EXERCISE

Regular exercise can improve mental health and reduce stress. Studies show that exercise reduces fatigue, improves alertness and concentration, and improves overall brain function. The benefits of exercise can help when stress and anxiety drain a person's energy or reduce the person's ability to concentrate. Exercise can also distract a person from fears and worries. When stressful feelings build, Jordan, who suffers from anxiety, finds that going to the gym to exercise helps him. "Mostly on

MEDITATION

For some, meditation is an effective way of calming the body and mind and reducing stress and tension. Meditation is the practice of using quieting or focusing techniques to train the mind to focus and redirect thoughts and become more aware of itself and the environment. This allows practitioners to become mentally clear and emotionally calm. There are many types of meditation. It can be as simple as pausing to focus on a few simple, controlled breaths. Teens can also learn to practice meditation from apps, classes, or meditation coaches. Several studies have shown that meditation may ease symptoms of anxiety and depression. It can also help relieve insomnia.

the treadmill or the bikes. Simple but slow workouts. I do it early in the a.m. If I start having an episode, walking or running in place helps," he says.[1]

Exercise produces endorphins, which are chemicals in the brain that act as natural painkillers. Endorphins also help a person sleep, which reduces stress. When the body feels better, the mind does as well. Researchers have found that regular aerobic exercise can decrease overall levels of tension, elevate mood, improve sleep, and improve self-esteem, according to the Anxiety and Depression Association of America (ADAA).

Even small amounts of exercise can help reduce anxiety symptoms. Researchers have found that the antianxiety effect of exercise begins to occur after only five minutes of aerobic exercise. In addition, psychologists studying the effects of exercise on anxiety and depression have found that walking for ten minutes can provide as much benefit as a 45-minute workout. Taking a brisk walk can reduce anxiety symptoms for several hours.

Other research has found evidence that people who are regularly physically active may have lower rates of anxiety and depression than people who are more sedentary. Regular exercise may help the brain deal more effectively with stress, which can improve mental health. In one study, researchers reported that people who regularly exercised vigorously were 25 percent less likely to develop an anxiety disorder or depression over the next five years than those who did not exercise regularly.[2]

HEALTHY EATING

Diet can also play an important role in managing anxiety symptoms. Eating a balanced diet and drinking enough water can help reduce these symptoms. When the brain does not have a steady supply of nutrients, it may not be able to produce neurotransmitters that are involved in

Eating healthful, balanced meals can help people
manage anxiety.

supporting mood and keeping the brain balanced, which
can lead to anxiety symptoms.

Along with following a healthy diet, eating certain foods
can help relieve anxiety. For example, the body metabolizes
complex carbohydrates more slowly than simple
carbohydrates. This allows the body to maintain a steadier
blood sugar level, which creates a calm feeling. As a result,
eating whole grains, vegetables, and fruits, which are rich
in complex carbohydrates, may benefit people with anxiety.
In addition, several specific foods have been shown to
reduce anxiety. Foods rich in zinc have been linked to lower

anxiety. These include oysters, cashews, beef, and egg yolks.

Researchers have shown in mice that diets low in magnesium increased anxiety behaviors. Therefore, magnesium-rich foods such as leafy greens, nuts, seeds, and whole grains may lower anxiety. Research has also shown that foods with omega-3 fatty acids such as salmon and other fatty fish may help reduce anxiety. Other specific foods that may help to reduce anxiety include asparagus and foods rich in vitamin B, such as almonds and avocados.

SUGAR AND ANXIETY

Having a sweet tooth may be harmful to a person's mental health. For people already dealing with anxiety, eating large amounts of processed sugar may trigger feelings of worry, sadness, and irritability. The rush of sugar in the bloodstream causes the body to work hard to get back in balance. The body releases the hormone insulin, which helps absorb the sugar in the blood and stabilize blood sugar levels. The rise and fall of blood sugar can leave a person feeling nervous, irritable, shaky, and tense. All of these side effects can make anxiety worse. In addition, excess sugar can weaken the body's ability to respond to stress, which can also make anxiety worse.

The timing of meals can affect anxiety symptoms. Skipping meals can cause large fluctuations in blood sugar levels, which can make people feel jittery, affect their mood, and worsen anxiety symptoms. Instead, eating small regular meals throughout the day can help

PROBIOTICS

Trillions of bacteria and other microorganisms live inside the human gut. Most of these microbes are beneficial and help the body's digestive and immune systems function efficiently. However, sometimes an imbalance in gut bacteria may cause certain physical symptoms such as digestive problems, bad breath, and autoimmune diseases. Research has also linked a healthy gut to brain health. Bacteria in the gut help produce several brain chemicals that help regulate mood, including serotonin. When the gut's healthy bacteria are out of balance, stress and anxiety can occur. Probiotics are supplements made from live, healthy bacteria that help maintain a healthy gut. Researchers are currently studying whether probiotics can be used to balance healthy gut bacteria and reduce anxiety symptoms.

to stabilize blood sugar levels and reduce anxiety symptoms.

Alcohol and caffeine can both trigger anxiety-like symptoms in the body. As a result, reducing intake of these substances can help people better manage their anxiety symptoms. Amanda, who suffers from anxiety, contributed to an article on health website the Mighty with advice from anxiety sufferers on day-to-day tricks to lower anxiety. Amanda wrote, "Cut out caffeine and drink more water. I was told by a therapist that it would help and it does. I noticed without the caffeine I don't feel as anxious. Not only does it help with my anxiety, but I know I'm hydrated."[4]

Setting a bedtime routine and avoiding screens before bed can help people get a full night's sleep.

THE IMPORTANCE OF SLEEP

During sleep, the body replenishes neurotransmitters necessary for supporting mood. Therefore, adequate sleep is essential for maintaining brain health and balance and for reducing anxiety. However, people with anxiety may find their racing thoughts and constant worries keep them up at night and interfere with their ability to get enough sleep. It becomes a negative cycle in which sleep deprivation can lead to an increase in anxiety symptoms, which in turn make sleep more difficult.

Doing yoga, meditating, and playing with pets are all activities that can relieve stress.

To get enough rest, some people find that sticking to a relaxing bedtime routine can improve sleep habits. They avoid stimulating substances such as caffeine and nicotine and turn off televisions and computers before bedtime. To relieve her anxiety, Niki, another contributor to the Mighty article on antianxiety habits, found that a routine has made getting a good night's sleep easier. She said, "[It] may sound silly, but after brushing teeth, etc., I wash my hands with a lavender soap. And use a good smell on my hands. Then climb into bed and take a few deep breaths. While repeating my mantra, 'You are physically, mentally, emotionally safe. The world is not out to get you. Nothing is as bad as it seems.' It really helps me."[5]

RELAX AND LOWER STRESS

Stress is one of the major factors contributing to all types of anxiety. As a result, many people find that active relaxation techniques such as yoga and meditation can help reduce stress and relieve anxiety symptoms. These activities allow a person to focus on a single task and push distracting anxieties out of the mind. Heidi Larson, a psychologist and professor of counseling and student development at Eastern Illinois University, studied how relaxation techniques can reduce test and academic anxiety in elementary school students. For the study, Larson designed a technique that involved a series of breathing and relaxation exercises. "We had students lie on mats on the floor of their classrooms. They closed their eyes and we asked them to focus on their breathing, then on tensing and relaxing groups of muscles in their legs, arms, stomachs and so on," Larson says. A control group of students at another school did not receive the relaxation exercises. When comparing the two groups of students, researchers found that the students who participated in the relaxation exercises showed a significant reduction in test anxiety compared to the students who did not participate.[6]

People may also turn to other less-structured activities to relieve stress. Some use art and writing as ways to release stress. Some play with pets, read, or listen to music. "I take my crochet with me everywhere I go now. It helps me while I sit and talk to people. Even if I'm not talking to someone, it can help bring a great conversation starter and helps ease my tension, as I keep my hands busy," Tatauq M. told the Mighty.[7]

ONLINE SUPPORT GROUPS

Online support groups offer another avenue for people with all types of anxiety to share their experiences. Online support groups are some of the easiest and most convenient ways for a person to find others dealing with the same problems. With only a computer and internet connection, participants can find a community and feel less isolated. When searching for an online support group, it is safer to look for a group affiliated with an established mental health organization. Mental health professionals may be able to recommend reputable online groups for patients. As with any online interaction, participants should be careful with how much personal information they share.

FINDING SUPPORT

Another key to managing anxiety is getting support. Support may come from family, friends, a good therapist, or a support group made up of people who have experienced anxiety. Sometimes just being around other people can help reduce symptoms. Many people find that joining a support group and meeting others with the same or similar experiences helps them manage their anxiety.

When Jake Heilbrunn was a college freshman,

he battled crippling anxiety. One day while meeting with a career counselor he trusted, Heilbrunn broke down crying in her office. "After bottling up my issues for months, I had found an adult who encouraged me to share what was on my mind. The relief I felt that day was enormous," he said. Over the next several months, Heilbrunn met with the counselor, and she taught him anxiety coping skills. Just being able to talk about his anxiety with a trusted adult made him feel better. He said:

> *Putting into words the anxious feelings that had been consuming me enabled me to listen to my feelings so they could inform me about my concerns. . . . I could begin figuring out what might help. These conversations changed the course of my life. They taught me that anxiety signals that there's a problem I need to address and solve. They kick-started my journey that led to me being able to overcome my disabling anxiety.*[8]

Lifestyle changes are not a cure for anxiety, but they can reduce contributing factors. Practices such as exercise, healthy eating, getting enough sleep, and reducing stress can help students better cope with their academic anxiety. Finding support in any form can also help teens learn how to live with academic anxiety.

Many schools are working to make the school environment less stressful for students.

CULTURE CHANGES TO COMBAT ACADEMIC ANXIETY

While school and everyday life can be challenging, dealing with academic anxiety is possible. The pressure on today's students, from elementary school to college, is intense. Yet schools and students are learning how to manage academic stress so that it does not become too overwhelming. "You don't have to be stressed . . . just because you're in a stressful environment. The key is learning how to soar through the stressors of [school] without becoming a stressed-out, burned-out mess," says former admissions adviser Kelci Lynn Lucier.[1]

CHANGING SCHOOL CULTURE

Today's students face incredibly busy days of classes, work, and activities followed by long nights of studying. The pressure to do it all well affects teens across the country. It is no surprise that anxiety has become one of the most common mental health challenges facing today's youth. Students constantly worry about tests, grades, and whether they will get into good colleges. In severe cases, anxiety interferes with daily life and affects teens' ability to do homework, hang out with friends, and participate in activities. Severe anxiety can also lead to depression and suicidal thoughts. As anxiety rises in schools across the country, educators are working to create school cultures and climates that understand the sources of student anxiety and help students develop the tools to manage anxiety.

At Lexington High School in Massachusetts, intense academic stress contributed to a student's suicide in 2017. The tragedy prompted the school district to make changes to a culture that overemphasized admission to Ivy League colleges. Today, students learn breathing exercises and study how tension affects the brain. New rules limit the amount of homework teachers can assign. Students are required to meet with guidance counselors when selecting classes to keep them from overscheduling themselves. To decrease competition among students, the school eliminated class rankings and does not name a valedictorian or salutatorian. The school has also implemented a 45-minute free period, which forces students to take time to relax.

The district's efforts also extend to the community by offering regular workshops on teen anxiety. Meetings about college admissions aim to convince parents that their children can succeed at non–Ivy League schools. "We are trying to change a culture that is deeply rooted

LATER START TIMES, LESS STRESS

Many students are exhausted, rising before dawn to get ready for school and staying up late after practices and work to finish hours of homework. Studies have shown that lack of sleep can affect people's mental health and put them at greater risk of developing anxiety. Some schools have pushed back start times to help students get more sleep. At Stevenson High School in Lincolnshire, Illinois, officials changed the school start time from 8:05 a.m. to 8:30 a.m. Parents and students have praised the 25-minute change and say it allows them a calmer start to the day. "It gives them time to connect with their teachers, connect with their friends or see people in student services if need be," says Sarah Bowen, director of student services at Stevenson High School. "They have time to get some extra sleep. We are starting to see some of the positive impact."[3]

FOUR-LEGGED FRIENDS

For many people, spending time with a pet can reduce stress, depression, and anxiety. According to the Anxiety and Depression Association of America, studies show "pets provide a sense of security and routine that [gives] emotional and social support."[6] Some animals are trained specifically to become therapy animals and help people experiencing stress. While dogs and cats are the most common therapy animals, other animals such as llamas and pigs can become therapy animals as well. Some schools are bringing therapy dogs to school to help improve student mental health and combat anxiety. For example, at Lane Tech College Prep school in Chicago, students snuggled with certified therapy dogs as a break from the stress of preparing for final exams. The school brings in dogs and volunteers from the Chicago-based Canine Therapy Corps to provide relief for stressed-out students.

here," says Lexington High School principal Laura Lasa.[4]

During freshman orientation, Lasa spoke to students about allowing themselves to make mistakes and learning how to reduce stress. "Do not believe that you must acquire straight A's to be a successful student," she said. "If you and/or your parents are caught up in society's picture of success, let us help you change the focus."[5]

TEACHING MINDFULNESS

Some schools are teaching students mindfulness to help them deal with

Many schools have begun teaching mindfulness techniques to help students manage anxiety.

academic pressure and anxiety. Mindfulness is a process of being aware of thoughts, feelings, body sensations, and environment without judgment. Research has shown that mindfulness can reduce anxiety by teaching a person how to respond to stress by being aware of his or her physical and mental state in the present moment. By focusing on the present, mindfulness can help a person reduce worrying about the future, which is a key part of anxiety.

At Roosevelt High School in Seattle, teachers who were alarmed by rising student anxiety instituted a daily 20-minute break in the schedule. Some days, students can use the 20-minute break to do what they want. Some relax, while others use the downtime to chat with friends or catch up on schoolwork. Once a week, teachers in every class use the 20-minute break to lead a lesson on mindfulness, teaching students how to be aware of their own thoughts and feelings in the moment. During one mindfulness lesson, history teacher Karen Grace led breathing exercises and talked with students about kindness. The lesson ended with a moment of silence, with the students closing their eyes and focusing on their breathing. The school hopes that the mindfulness lessons will give students the tools to manage anxiety and focus on things beyond academics.

Beyond the 20-minute break, some teachers use mindfulness exercises regularly throughout the day. Before a test,

TRY A MINDFULNESS EXERCISE

There are many different types of mindfulness exercises that can help ease anxiety symptoms. One example starts with finding a comfortable position, such as sitting upright in a chair with feet resting comfortably on the ground or sitting cross-legged on the floor. Once in a good position, the person relaxes his gaze and lowers his chin toward his chest. At the same time, the person concentrates on breathing and focuses on the air as it moves through the nose and out the mouth. Some people choose to silently repeat a calming word or phrase. Beginners often start meditating with short daily sessions, about five to ten minutes. As people become more experienced with meditation, they may gradually meditate for longer sessions.

Grace has students write what they are worried about and then crush the paper and throw it in the trash. This practice helps students visualize their worries and fears differently, Grace says. The focus on mindfulness and emotional health appears to be helping reduce academic pressure and anxiety throughout the school. Teachers and students report that the entire school feels calmer. "I think it's changed the tone of how we get through the day," Grace says. "It's still fast-paced, but it's sane and reasonable."[7]

LIVING SUCCESSFULLY WITH ACADEMIC ANXIETY

Managing anxiety can be challenging. Anxiety is a chronic condition with symptoms that ebb and flow. However, many teens learn

ATTENTION BIAS MODIFICATION TREATMENT

Mental health professionals are testing a new treatment for children and teens with anxiety called attention bias modification treatment. This therapy is based on the idea that youths and adults with anxiety are overly focused on potentially threatening stimuli in their environment. Some researchers are testing a gamelike computer training program that teaches kids to focus on neutral stimuli and ignore threatening stimuli. The therapy appears to have promise. According to a study published in 2019, researchers found that teens who received attention bias modification treatment showed significant decreases in anxiety severity.[8]

With help and support, teens can overcome academic anxiety to live joyful, less stressful lives.

how to manage their anxiety and reduce stress through a combination of approaches including psychotherapy, lifestyle changes, medication, and relaxation techniques. They surround themselves with a strong support system to help during difficult times and educate themselves about anxiety and its effect on the body and mind.

When dealing with academic anxiety, patience is essential. Because anxiety affects each person differently, it may take some time to find the right method or combination of methods that lessen symptoms. Esther's story shows how patience and persistence can lead to success. During graduate school, Esther developed intense academic anxiety, which caused her to faint, vomit, and avoid social activity. She constantly worried about disappointing friends and family. Eventually, she reached out for help at the school's counseling center. "I found that a combination of a mindfulness course, intensive counseling, and a transition away from grad school to more predictable full-time employment has started to help," she says. "Over the past year, I have made a lot of time to look after myself. It hasn't been constant improvement, more cyclical in nature. I still have the occasional sleepless night . . . or anxious morning, but I've gotten to know myself a lot better." Esther knows that her anxiety may come back in the future, but she feels confident that she will be able to handle it. "I've developed the tools to deal with those situations when they arise," she says.[9]

Academic pressure and the anxiety it causes affects students across the country. Living with anxiety is never easy. However, understanding what academic anxiety is, what causes it, how it affects daily life, and how to get help are the first steps in overcoming anxiety and leading a full and productive life.

"THE BEST THING WE CAN DO IS REALLY GIVING THESE KIDS THE TYPES OF PROGRAMS TO TEACH THEM TO COPE."[10]
—BO PAULLE, SOCIOLOGY PROFESSOR AT THE UNIVERSITY OF AMSTERDAM

FACTS ABOUT ACADEMIC ANXIETY

- Anxiety is the body's natural response to stress. Severe anxiety can develop into an anxiety disorder. Anxiety disorders are the most common mental health conditions in the United States.

- In 2018, 61 percent of teens said they felt "a lot" of pressure to get good grades, while an additional 27 percent said they felt "some" pressure to get good grades.

- Academic anxiety is not a clinical disorder but is included as part of generalized anxiety disorder or social anxiety disorder.

IMPACT ON DAILY LIFE

- Academic anxiety can have a negative effect on a student's academic performance and make it difficult to focus.

- Academic anxiety can increase negative thoughts, which can lower a student's self-esteem.

- People with academic anxiety may experience unpleasant physical symptoms.

- Academic anxiety can lead to other mental health issues such as depression and suicidal thoughts.

DEALING WITH ACADEMIC ANXIETY

- The earlier anxiety is detected, the more effective treatment can be.

- Cognitive behavioral therapy (CBT) is a common type of psychotherapy used to treat anxiety disorders.

- Improving study skills and learning time management can reduce academic anxiety.

- Lifestyle changes such as regular exercise, healthy eating, adequate sleep, and reduced stress can lower anxiety symptoms.

- Finding support is a key component of managing academic anxiety.

- Some schools are working to change school culture and help students develop tools to manage academic anxiety.

QUOTE

"It comes down to balance. You can't be 'on' 24/7. How can you allocate some time to an activity that can help relieve stress?"

—*Mary Alvord, a psychologist specializing in teens*

amygdala

A region of the brain that processes emotionally charged memories, including fear, and plays a role in the early stages of extinguishing embedded fears.

cortisol

A hormone that is involved in the fight-or-flight response to a perceived threat.

diagnose

To have symptoms classified as a disease or condition, usually by a medical professional.

empathy

Being able to understand and share another person's thoughts and feelings.

gene

A unit of hereditary information found in a chromosome.

hormone

A regulatory substance that sparks an action, such as growth, digestion, or sexual maturation, in a tissue or organ.

neurotransmitter

A brain chemical that helps brain cells communicate with other brain cells.

perfectionist

A person who wants everything to be perfect and demands the highest standards possible.

salutatorian

The student with the second-highest grade in a graduating class.

serotonin

A neurotransmitter involved in regulating moods, sleep, and appetite, and in inhibiting pain.

thyroid

A large gland in the neck that secretes hormones that regulate how fast the body uses energy and how the body grows and develops.

valedictorian

The student with the highest grade in a graduating class.

SELECTED BIBLIOGRAPHY

"Anxiety Disorders." *NAMI*, Dec. 2017, nami.org. Accessed
23 June 2020.

Flannery, Mary Ellen. "The Epidemic of Anxiety among
Today's Students." *NEA Today*, 28 Mar. 2018, neatoday.org.
Accessed 23 June 2020.

FURTHER READINGS

Bernstein, Jeffrey. *Mindfulness for Teen Worry: Quick and
Easy Strategies to Let Go of Anxiety, Worry, and Stress.* New
Harbinger, 2018.

Buckey, A. W. *Dealing with Anxiety Disorder.*
ReferencePoint, 2020.

Cik, Kate F. *Anxiety: The Ultimate Teen Guide.* Rowman &
Littlefield, 2020.

ONLINE RESOURCES

To learn more about academic anxiety,
please visit **abdobooklinks.com** or scan this
QR code. These links are routinely
monitored and updated to provide the most
current information available.

MORE INFORMATION

For more information on this subject, contact or visit the following organizations:

Anxiety and Depression Association of America (ADAA)

8701 Georgia Ave., Ste. 412
Silver Spring, MD 20910
240-485-1001
adaa.org

The ADAA is a national nonprofit that provides information on anxiety and depression treatment options.

National Alliance on Mental Illness (NAMI)

4301 Wilson Blvd., Ste. 300
Arlington, VA 22203
703-524-7600
nami.org

NAMI works to educate, advocate, listen, and lead to improve the lives of people with mental illness and their loved ones.

SOURCE NOTES

CHAPTER 1. TEST TIME

1. Karen Ann Cullotta et al. "'No Worse Fate than Failure': How Pressure to Keep Up Is Overwhelming Students in Elite Districts." *Chicago Tribune*, 13 Nov. 2017, chicagotribune.com. Accessed 26 Aug. 2020.
2. Juliana Menasce Horowitz and Nikki Graf. "Most US Teens See Anxiety and Depression as a Major Problem among Their Peers." *Pew Research Center*, 20 Feb. 2019, pewsocialtrends.org. Accessed 26 Aug. 2020.
3. Horowitz and Graf, "Most US Teens See Anxiety and Depression."
4. Benoit Denizet-Lewis. "Why Are More American Teenagers than Ever Suffering from Severe Anxiety?" *New York Times Magazine*, 11 Oct. 2017, nytimes.com. Accessed 26 Aug. 2020.
5. Mary Ellen Flannery. "The Epidemic of Anxiety among Today's Students." *NEA Today*, 28 Mar. 2018, neatoday.org. Accessed 26 Aug. 2020.
6. "What Stresses You Out about School?" *TeensHealth*, 2020, kidshealth.org. Accessed 26 Aug. 2020.

CHAPTER 2. WHAT IS ACADEMIC ANXIETY?

1. Sophie Stephens. "Test Anxiety." *West Side Story*, 8 Dec. 2017, wsspaper.com. Accessed 26 Aug. 2020.
2. "Anxiety Disorders." *NAMI*, Dec. 2017, nami.org. Accessed 26 Aug. 2020.
3. Hossein Sharif. "Suneung: The Day Silence Falls over South Korea." *BBC*, 26 Nov. 2018, bbc.com. Accessed 26 Aug. 2020.
4. Mary Ellen Flannery. "The Epidemic of Anxiety among Today's Students." *NEA Today*, 28 Mar. 2018, neatoday.org. Accessed 26 Aug. 2020.
5. Rebecca Dillon. "Maths Anxiety." *My Student Teacher Story*, 6 Nov. 2017, blogs.glowscotland.org.uk. Accessed 26 Aug. 2020.
6. Sarah Hanson. "Academic Anxiety: How Perfectionism and Executive Dysfunction Collide." *Beyond BookSmart*, 6 June 2016, beyondbooksmart.com. Accessed 26 Aug. 2020.
7. Hanson, "Academic Anxiety."
8. Alice Yin. "Coping with Teenage Anxiety: Readers Share Their Stories." *New York Times Magazine*, 23 Oct. 2017, nytimes.com. Accessed 26 Aug. 2020.
9. Yin, "Coping with Teenage Anxiety."
10. A. Pawlowski. "Generation Stress? How Anxiety Rules the Secret Life of Teens." *Today*, 17 Sept. 2014, today.com. Accessed 26 Aug. 2020.

CHAPTER 3. SIGNS AND SYMPTOMS

1. Perri Klass. "Helping Students with Test Anxiety." *New York Times*, 24 June 2019, nytimes.com. Accessed 26 Aug. 2020.
2. A. Pawlowski. "Generation Stress? How Anxiety Rules the Secret Life of Teens." *Today*, 17 Sept. 2014, today.com. Accessed 26 Aug. 2020.
3. "Class of 2019." *CollegeBoard*, 2020, reports.collegeboard.org. Accessed 26 Aug. 2020.

4. Lucy Dwyer. "When Anxiety Hits at School." *Atlantic*, 3 Oct. 2014, theatlantic.com. Accessed 26 Aug. 2020.

5. Rachel Ehmke. "Anxiety in the Classroom." *Child Mind Institute*, 2020, childmind.org. Accessed 26 Aug. 2020.

6. Ehmke, "Anxiety in the Classroom."

7. Susan Donaldson James. "Mental Health Problems Rising among College Students." *NBC News*, 28 June 2017, nbcnews.com. Accessed 26 Aug. 2020.

8. Jenny Brundin. "Teen Diary: Amelia Tells Us How Academic Stress Led Her to a Breakdown." *CPR News*, 2 Dec. 2019, cpr.org. Accessed 26 Aug. 2020.

9. Marcia Morris. "Mom, I'm Having a Panic Attack." *Psychology Today*, 26 Mar. 2016, psychologytoday.com. Accessed 26 Aug. 2020.

10. Joel Brown. "Anxiety and Depression." *BU Today*, 2 Oct. 2016, bu.edu. Accessed 26 Aug. 2020.

11. Brown, "Anxiety and Depression."

12. Michele DiGirolamo. "How to Overcome Test Anxiety in College." *AC Online*, 2020, affordablecollegesonline.org. Accessed 26 Aug. 2020.

CHAPTER 4. CAUSES OF ACADEMIC ANXIETY

1. Tim Walker. "Educators Look to Parents and Communities to Help Reduce Student Stress." *NEA Today*, 16 Sept. 2016, neatoday.org. Accessed 26 Aug. 2020.

2. "Anxiety Disorders." *NIH*, n.d., nimh.nih.gov. Accessed 26 Aug. 2020.

3. Kate Thayer. "School Brings in Therapy Dogs to Ease Students' Stress before Exams." *Daily World*, 29 Jan. 2019, thedailyworld.com. Accessed 26 Aug. 2020.

4. Karen Ann Cullotta et al. "'No Worse Fate than Failure': How Pressure to Keep Up Is Overwhelming Students in Elite Districts." *Chicago Tribune*, 13 Nov. 2017, chicagotribune.com. Accessed 26 Aug. 2020.

5. Cullotta et al., "'No Worse Fate than Failure.'"

6. Walker, "Educators Look to Parents and Communities."

7. Dan Peters. "A Message from Dr. Dan Peters: Managing Anxiety in Gifted Children." *Summit Center*, 2 July 2012, summitcenter.us. Accessed 26 Aug. 2020.

8. Paula Prober. "I Have to Know It before I Learn It—A Gifted Kid's Conundrum." *Your Rainforest Mind*, 30 July 2018, rainforestmind.wordpress.com. Accessed 26 Aug. 2020.

CHAPTER 5. EFFECTS ON DAILY LIFE

1. Valerie Strauss. "Test Anxiety: Why It Is Increasing and 3 Ways to Curb It." *Washington Post*, 10 Feb. 2013, washingtonpost.com. Accessed 26 Aug. 2020.

2. "American College Health Association-National College Health Assessment II: Reference Group Executive Summary Spring 2019." *American College Health Association*, 2019, acha.org. Accessed 26 Aug. 2020.

3. Katie Reilly. "Record Numbers of College Students Are Seeking Treatment for Depression and Anxiety—But Schools Can't Keep Up." *Time*, 19 Mar. 2018, time.com. Accessed 26 Aug. 2020.

4. Tim Walker. "Educators Look to Parents and Communities to Help Reduce Student Stress." *NEA Today*, 16 Sept. 2016, neatoday.org. Accessed 26 Aug. 2020.

5. Kenneth Shore. "The Student with Low Self-Esteem." *Education World*, 2020, educationworld.com. Accessed 26 Aug. 2020.

6. Cassie Shortsleeve. "11 Physical Symptoms of Anxiety, because It's Not All Mental." *Self*, 18 July 2020, self.com. Accessed 26 Aug. 2020.

7. Shortsleeve, "11 Physical Symptoms of Anxiety, because It's Not All Mental."

8. Haley Tiffany. "A Day in the Life of a Student with an Anxiety Disorder." *Teen Vogue*, 4 Feb. 2017, teenvogue.com. Accessed 26 Aug. 2020.

9. Walker, "Educators Look to Parents and Communities."

10. Thomas Tjornehoj. "The Relationship between Anxiety and Depression." *Hartgrove Behavioral Health System*, 2020, hartgrovehospital.com. Accessed 26 Aug. 2020.

11. "Treating Addiction with Anxiety Disorders." *American Addiction Centers*, 3 Feb. 2020, americanaddictioncenters.org. Accessed 26 Aug. 2020.

12. Hanna Rosin. "The Silicon Valley Suicides." *Atlantic*, Dec. 2015, theatlantic.com. Accessed 26 Aug. 2020.

CHAPTER 6. OVERCOMING ACADEMIC ANXIETY

1. "What Is Anxiety and How to Overcome It." *Get Schooled*, 23 Aug. 2020, getschooled.com. Accessed 26 Aug. 2020.

2. Alice Yin. "Coping with Teenage Anxiety: Readers Share Their Stories." *New York Times Magazine*, 23 Oct. 2017, nytimes.com. Accessed 26 Aug. 2020.

3. Diana Rodriquez. "Overcoming College Test Anxiety." *Everyday Health*, 17 Mar. 2010, everydayhealth.com. Accessed 26 Aug. 2020.

4. Leah Shafer. "Resilience for Anxious Students." *Harvard Graduate School of Education*, 30 Nov. 2017, gse.harvard.edu. Accessed 26 Aug. 2020.

5. Shafer, "Resilience for Anxious Students."

6. Shafer, "Resilience for Anxious Students."

7. Sarah Schuster. "17 'Small,' but Significant, Lifestyle Changes that Help People with Anxiety." *Mighty*, 3 Apr. 2018, themighty.com. Accessed 26 Aug. 2020.

8. Michaele Charles. "Getting Past Test Anxiety." *Front Range Community College*, 20 Sept. 2011, blog.frontrange.edu. Accessed 26 Aug. 2020.

9. Joel Brown. "Anxiety and Depression." *BU Today*, 2 Oct. 2016, bu.edu. Accessed 26 Aug. 2020.

10. Brown, "Anxiety and Depression."

11. Brown, "Anxiety and Depression."

CHAPTER 7. LIVING WITH LESS STRESS

1. Sarah Schuster. "17 'Small,' but Significant, Lifestyle Changes that Help People with Anxiety." *Mighty*, 3 Apr. 2018, themighty.com. Accessed 26 Aug. 2020.
2. "Exercise for Stress and Anxiety." *Anxiety and Depression Association of America*, 2020, adaa.org. Accessed 26 Aug. 2020.
3. Alexandra Ossola. "High-Stress High School." *Atlantic*, 9 Oct. 2015, theatlantic.com. Accessed 26 Aug. 2020.
4. Schuster, "Lifestyle Changes That Help People with Anxiety."
5. Schuster, "Lifestyle Changes That Help People with Anxiety."
6. Valerie Strauss. "Test Anxiety: Why It Is Increasing and 3 Ways to Curb It." *Washington Post*, 10 Feb. 2013, washingtonpost.com. Accessed 26 Aug. 2020.
7. Schuster, "Lifestyle Changes That Help People with Anxiety."
8. Susan Heitler. "High School and College Student Anxiety: Why the Epidemic?" *Psychology Today*, 21 June 2018, psychologytoday.com. Accessed 26 Aug. 2020.

CHAPTER 8. CULTURE CHANGES TO COMBAT ACADEMIC ANXIETY

1. Kelci Lynn Lucier. "College Stress Solutions for Academic Anxiety." *Collegexpress*, 25 Apr. 2014, collegexpress.com. Accessed 26 Aug. 2020.
2. Tim Walker. "Educators Look to Parents and Communities to Help Reduce Student Stress." *NEA Today*, 16 Sept. 2016, neatoday.org. Accessed 26 Aug. 2020.
3. Karen Ann Cullotta et al. "Later Start Times, Less Homework: Here's What Elite Schools Are Doing to Help Students Cope with Stress." *Chicago Tribune*, 14 Nov. 2017, chicagotribune.com. Accessed 26 Aug. 2020.
4. Kyle Spencer. "It Takes a Suburb: A Town Struggles to Ease Student Stress." *New York Times*, 5 Apr. 2017, nytimes.com. Accessed 26 Aug. 2020.
5. Spencer, "It Takes a Suburb."
6. Steven Feldman. "Alleviating Anxiety, Stress and Depression with the Pet Effect." *Anxiety and Depression Association of America*, 2020, adaa.org. Accessed 26 Aug. 2020.
7. Paige Cornwell. "Schools Create Moments of Calm for Stressed-Out Students." *Seattle Times*, 10 Dec. 2016, seattletimes.com. Accessed 26 Aug. 2020.
8. Emily Pond. "Attention Bias Modification Treatment Effective for Treatment-Resistant Anxiety in Youth." *Psychiatry Advisor*, 23 Apr. 2019, psychiatryadvisor.com. Accessed 26 Aug. 2020.
9. Esther R. "My Struggle with Anxiety During Grad School." *Anxiety Canada*, 17 May 2017, anxietycanada.com. Accessed 26 Aug. 2020.
10. Alexandra Ossola. "High-Stress High School." *Atlantic*, 9 Oct. 2015, theatlantic.com. Accessed 26 Aug. 2020.

INDEX

ABOUT THE AUTHOR

CARLA MOONEY

Carla Mooney is the author of many books for young adults and children. She lives in Pittsburgh, Pennsylvania, with her husband and three children.

ABOUT THE CONSULTANT

JERRELL C. CASSADY, PhD

Jerrell C. Cassady, PhD, is a professor of psychology in the Department of Educational Psychology at Ball State University. He is also the director of the Academic Anxiety Resource Center. Dr. Cassady has been researching test anxiety and academic anxiety for more than 25 years, promoting methods of identifying and treating students with academic anxieties. His book *Anxiety in Schools: The Causes, Consequences, and Solutions for Academic Anxieties* was the first comprehensive focus on the notion of academic anxiety as a condition and addresses various forms of academic anxieties (e.g., test anxiety, reading anxiety, math anxiety). He is the associate editor of the journal *Anxiety, Stress, and Coping*.